THE MIAMI HEAT

BY

MARK STEWART

Content Consultant
Matt Zeysing
Historian and Archivist
The Naismith Memorial Basketball Hall of Fame

NORWOOD HOUSE PRESS
CHICAGO, ILLINOIS

Norwood House Press
P.O. Box 316598
Chicago, Illinois 60631

For information regarding Norwood House Press, please visit our website at:
www.norwoodhousepress.com or call 866-565-2900.

All photos courtesy of AP/Wide World Photos, Inc. except the following:
Topps, Inc. (6, 14, 21, 40, 43); Author's Collection (34);
Eliot J. Schechter/Getty Images (cover image).
Special thanks to Topps, Inc.

Editor: Mike Kennedy
Designer: Ron Jaffe
Project Management: Black Book Partners, LLC.

Special thanks to Nancy Volkman

Library of Congress Cataloging-in-Publication Data

Stewart, Mark, 1960-
The Miami Heat / by Mark Stewart, with content consultant Matt Zeysing.
      p. cm. -- (Team spirit)
   Summary: "Presents the history, accomplishments and key personalities of
the Miami Heat basketball team. Includes timelines, quotes, maps, glossary
and websites"--Provided by publisher.
   Includes bibliographical references and index.
   ISBN-13: 978-1-59953-009-3 (library edition : alk. paper)
   ISBN-10: 1-59953-009-0 (library edition : alk. paper) 1. Miami Heat
(Basketball team)--Juvenile literature. I. Zeysing, Matt. II. Title. III. Series.
   GV885.52.M53S84 2006
   796.323'6409759381--dc22
                                                                  2005034376

Manufactured in the United States of America.

COVER PHOTO: The Miami Heat gather for a team meeting during a 2005 game.

Table of Contents

SPORTS WORDS & VOCABULARY WORDS: In this book, you will find many words that are new to you. You may also see familiar words used in new ways. The glossary on page 46 gives the meanings of basketball words, as well as "everyday" words that have special basketball meanings. These words appear in **bold type** throughout the book. The glossary on page 47 gives the meanings of vocabulary words that are not related to basketball. They appear in ***bold italic type*** throughout the book.

BASKETBALL SEASONS: Because each basketball season begins late in one year and ends early in the next, seasons are not named after years. Instead, they are written out as two years separated by a dash, for example 1944–45 or 2005–06.

Meet the Heat

There is no such thing as a guaranteed win in basketball. The best chance is to play good, hard nose-to-nose defense. The Miami Heat have made this their team *tradition*. They are "in your face" from the opening **tip-off** to the final buzzer. Their goal is to keep opponents from putting the ball in the basket every time down the court.

If you find a way to score against the Heat, they will find a new way to stop you. If you challenge the Heat, they simply will not back down. Miami may be a *laid-back* city, but once you step inside the team's arena, it is a very different world.

This book tells the story of the Heat. Although they have only been around since 1988, the team and its fans have had plenty of time to form a close bond. Miami has shown its players a lot of love over the years. The Heat have repaid this support with the kind of effort that makes fans cheer and makes coaches proud.

Alonzo Mourning greets Antoine Walker as he comes off the court. The Heat have mixed experienced players like these with exciting young players to become one of the top teams in the NBA.

Way Back When

The Miami area is known for many things. Its lovely palm trees, grand hotels, long beaches, and warm waters are famous all over the world. Miami is also known as one of America's liveliest sports towns—although this was not always the case. For many years, the city was home to only one professional team, the Miami Dolphins. In the 1980s, the **National Basketball Association (NBA)** announced that it would be adding new teams. Miami's sports fans wanted to make sure they got one.

BILLY CUNNINGHAM   FORWARD

Billy Cunningham

The city's *campaign* for an NBA team was led by Zev Buffman, Billy Cunningham, and Ted Arison. Buffman was a man who had become wealthy in the entertainment business. Cunningham was a former NBA player and coach who had always dreamed of owning a team. Arison owned a cruise ship line and *invested* in *real estate*—his son, Mickey, would later run the team. These men convinced the NBA that Miami was the perfect place to

put a new team. The Heat joined the league for the 1988–89 season.

The Heat struggled, losing their first 17 games in a row. No team in any sport has ever started this poorly. They got better as the season went on, but finished with just 15 victories. There was one good thing about being so bad. In the NBA, the teams that lose the most get to pick first from the best college players each spring. Over the next few years, the Heat lost a lot of games, but they were able to build a competitive team. Their young stars included Glen Rice, Steve Smith, Grant Long, Sherman Douglas, and Rony Seikaly.

The final pieces of the puzzle came together during the 1995–96 season. Pat Riley was hired to coach the team and center Alonzo Mourning joined the Heat. Midway through the season, Miami traded for Tim Hardaway, a lightning-quick point guard. The difference in the team was amazing. A year later, the Heat won 61 games and fell just short of making it to the **NBA Finals**.

Once the Heat found a winning formula, they began to *acquire* players who fit in with their style. They won by playing rugged defense and wearing down their opponents. Their victories were not always "pretty," but Heat fans appreciated their hard-working players. When opponents came to Miami, they knew they would be in for the fight of their lives.

LEFT: Pat Riley celebrates on the sidelines during a Miami victory.
TOP: Alonzo Mourning shows the emotion that he brought to the team in 1995.

Home Court

The Heat play their home games in American Airlines Arena, which opened during the 1999–2000 season. The first game was played on January 2, 2000. Because many entertainers have homes in the Miami area, the Heat's arena is a good place to go "star-gazing." Some of the world's most famous actors and musicians can be seen sitting among the fans at Heat games.

For those who like to keep their eyes on the court, the Heat have one of the NBA's most popular mascots. His name is Burnie and he likes to clown around with the fans. The Heat's dance team is also one of the best in the league.

AMERICAN AIRLINES ARENA BY THE NUMBERS

- *American Airlines Arena has 19,600 seats.*
- *The arena cost $175 million to build.*
- *The Heat won the first game ever played in the arena. They beat the Orlando Magic 111–103.*

The Rockets meet the Heat on Miami's home court.

Dressed for Success

The Heat uniform has always been "hot." The T in HEAT on the uniform top has flames trailing off it. Miami's shorts have a flaming basketball going through a hoop. This is also the team's official logo.

The Heat's colors are black, red and white. They have always used these colors in their uniform. At home, the team wears white jerseys and shorts. On the road, they wear black jerseys and shorts.

Both uniforms have red striping that runs straight down under the arms and along the sides of the shorts.

Like many NBA teams, the Heat have more than two uniform styles. Their third uniform is fire red. They wear this uniform for special occasions only.

Sherman Douglas fires a pass wearing Miami's first road uniform. The design has changed little over the years.

UNIFORM BASICS

The basketball uniform is very simple. It consists of a roomy top and baggy shorts.

- The top hangs from the shoulders, with big "scoops" for the arms and neck. This style has not changed much over the years.

- Shorts, however, have changed a lot. They used to be very short, so players could move their legs freely. In the last 20 years, shorts have actually gotten longer and much baggier.

Basketball uniforms look the same as they did long ago...until you look very closely. In the old days, the shorts had belts and buckles. The tops were made of a thick cotton called "jersey," which got very heavy when players sweated. Later, uniforms were made of shiny **satin**. They may have looked great, but they did not "breathe." Players got very hot! Today, most uniforms are made of **synthetic** materials that soak up sweat and keep the body cool.

Shaquille O'Neal runs down the court in Miami's home uniform.

We Won!

At the start of each season, Miami fans dream of winning a championship. In the Heat's first 17 seasons, they could not make this dream come true. Still, the team has scored some amazing victories over the years.

During the 1996–97 season, the Heat finished first in their **division**. To reach the NBA Finals, they needed to beat Michael Jordan and the Chicago Bulls. But first they had to overcome challenges from the Orlando Magic and New York Knicks. The Heat had fierce rivalries with both teams.

Miami and Orlando are Florida's two NBA cities, so there is always a little extra *at stake* when they play. This series was even until the final quarter of the **deciding game**. The Heat won with the help of their home crowd, and advanced to the next round of playoffs.

Tim Hardaway leads the cheers during a Miami playoff victory.

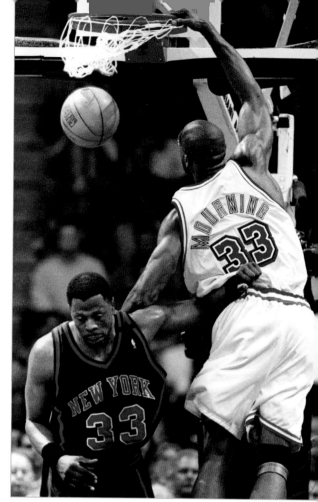

Alonzo Mourning dunks over Patrick Ewing of the Knicks in one of their playoff battles.

The Heat players were exhausted when they began their series with the Knicks. New York took advantage of this and won three of the first four games. The Heat, however, refused to lose. They won the next two games to tie the series at three victories each. In Game Seven, Tim Hardaway was unstoppable. He scored 38 points to lead Miami to a 101–90 victory.

Very few teams in history have won a series after being behind three games to one, but the Heat made it happen. Unfortunately, Miami had nothing left when it came time to play the Bulls. They could win only one game against the defending NBA champions.

During the 2004–05 season, the Heat came even closer to the NBA Finals. They beat the New Jersey Nets in the first round of the playoffs. Then they faced the Washington Wizards in the second round. The Wizards put up a great battle, but Shaquille O'Neal and

Dwyane Wade were too much for Washington to handle. In the final game of the series, Wade hit shots from all over the court and finished with 42 points. It was one of the best performances in team history.

The Heat played the Detroit Pistons for a chance to go to the NBA Finals. It looked as if they would make it until a leg injury slowed down O'Neal. Wade tried to carry the team to victory, but he was injured, too. The Pistons won the series four games to three. Although Miami fans were disappointed, they left the arena after the last game hungrier than ever for a championship.

ABOVE: Dwyane Wade and Alonzo Mourning sandwich Larry Hughes during a 2005 playoff game against the Wizards. **RIGHT**: Alonzo Mourning blocks a shot by Gilbert Arenas of the Wizards during the 2005 playoffs.

Go-To Guys

To be a true star in the NBA, you need more than a great shot. You have to be a "go-to guy"—someone teammates trust to make the winning play when the seconds are ticking away in a big game. Miami fans have had a lot to cheer about over the years, including these great stars...

THE PIONEERS

RONY SEIKALY · 6' 11" Center

• BORN: 5/10/1965   • PLAYED FOR TEAM: 1988–89 TO 1993–1994

Rony Seikaly was the Heat's first college draft pick. He was born in Beirut, Lebanon, and grew up in Greece. He attended Syracuse University in New York, but the Miami fans adopted him as their own.

GRANT LONG · 6' 9" Forward

• BORN: 3/12/1966   • PLAYED FOR TEAM: 1988–89 TO 1994–95

Grant Long was a multi-talented player who did whatever the Heat asked of him. He could score near the basket, grab rebounds against bigger opponents, play good defense, and be a strong leader.

SHERMAN DOUGLAS   6' 0" Guard

- BORN: 9/15/1966   • PLAYED FOR TEAM: 1989–90 TO 1991–92

Sherman Douglas was the team's first great **point guard**. He was an excellent passer and shooter. In his second year with with the Heat, Douglas led the team in points, **assists**, and **shooting percentage**.

GLEN RICE   6' 7" Forward

- BORN: 5/28/1967

- PLAYED FOR TEAM: 1989–90 TO 1994–95

Glen Rice was the best shooter in team history. No shot was out of his range, especially beyond the **3-point line**. Five times in his six seasons with the Heat, he **averaged** more than 20 points per game.

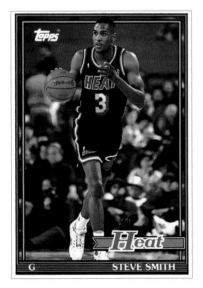

STEVE SMITH   6' 7" Guard

- BORN: 3/31/1969

- FIRST PLAYED FOR TEAM: 1991–92 TO 1994–1995

- RETURNED TO TEAM: 2004–05

Steve Smith was the Heat's first "do-it-all" star. He could pass and shoot like a guard, **drive** to the hoop like a forward, and rebound like a center.

LEFT: Steve Smith   **TOP**: Glen Rice

ALONZO MOURNING   6' 10" Center

- BORN: 2/8/1970   • FIRST PLAYED FOR TEAM: 1995–96 TO 2001–02
- RETURNED TO TEAM: 2004–05

Mourning was the fiercest player ever to wear a Miami uniform. He was a great defender and shot-blocker, and a dangerous scorer, too. Mourning was named NBA Defensive Player of the Year in 1999 and 2000.

TIM HARDAWAY   6' 0" Guard

- BORN: 9/1/1966
- PLAYED FOR TEAM: 1995–96 TO 2000–01

Tim Hardaway could change a game with his speed, toughness, and intelligence. When he was hot, he was almost impossible to stop. Hardaway always wanted the ball in his hands with the game on the line.

P.J. BROWN   6' 11" Forward

- BORN: 10/14/1969   • PLAYED FOR TEAM: 1996–97 TO 1999–00

P.J. Brown did not score a lot of points, but he was one of the best rebounders and defenders in the league in the 1990s. Miami won four division titles in the four years Brown was on the team.

EDDIE JONES   6' 6" Guard

- BORN: 10/20/1971
- PLAYED FOR TEAM: 2000–01 TO 2004–05

Eddie Jones was known for his defense when he came into the NBA. By the time he joined the Heat, he had become an excellent scorer, too.

DWYANE WADE   6' 4" Guard

- BORN: 1/17/1982 • FIRST SEASON WITH TEAM: 2003–04

Dwyane Wade was expected to be a good NBA player when the Heat drafted him in 2003. He turned out to be great. In just his second season, Wade played in the **All-Star Game** and was voted **All-NBA**.

SHAQUILLE O'NEAL   7' 1" Center

- BORN: 3/6/1972 • FIRST SEASON WITH TEAM: 2004–05

When the Heat traded for Shaquille O'Neal, they let the NBA know that they had their sights set on a championship. In his first year with Miami, "Shaq" turned the Heat into one of the best teams in basketball.

On the Sidelines

The Heat have always had excellent people running their team. Billy Cunningham, who helped bring the Heat to Miami, won NBA championships both as a player and and as a coach. He also was the Most Valuable Player of the **American Basketball Association (ABA)** during the 1972–73 season. Cunningham was elected to the **Hall of Fame** in 1986.

In 1991–92, the Heat asked Kevin Loughery to coach the team. Like Cunningham, Loughery had been a star in the NBA. He had been a scout for the Heat, so he knew his players very well. Loughery convinced them that they could win games with hard work and hustle. Under Loughery, the Heat made the playoffs twice.

In 1995–96, Pat Riley became the team's coach. Under Riley, the Heat finished first in its division four years in a row, and won 61 games in 1996–97. Riley retired from coaching for health reasons, but continued to help run the team. His replacement, Stan Van Gundy, coached the Heat to within a single win of the NBA Finals. When Riley returned to health, he agreed to come back and coach Miami during the 2005–06 season.

When Pat Riley is on the sidelines, there is no question who is in charge.

One Great Day

Heat fans did not have much to cheer about during the 1992–93 season. The club went 36–46 and failed to make the playoffs. The team did have some flashy young players, including Glen Rice and Harold Miner. But it was one of Miami's least exciting players, Brian Shaw, who gave fans the biggest thrill that year.

Shaw was a **role player**. His specialties were defense and passing. Shaw played when the Heat needed someone to guard a good shooter, or when they wanted an extra **playmaker** in the game. Scoring points and launching long jumpshots were not his jobs. For one magical night, however, Shaw was the greatest shooter the game has ever known.

The Heat were playing the Milwaukee Bucks, and Shaw surprised everyone when he tried a 3-point shot early in the first quarter. Even more surprising was that the ball touched nothing but net. Shaw's teammates got him the ball again, and again he put one in from far outside. By the end of the quarter, he had six 3-pointers.

Brian Shaw gives his teammates the "thumbs-up" sign.

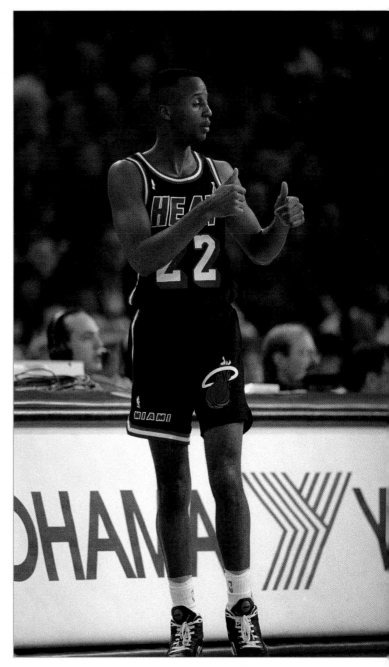

In the third quarter, Shaw found himself open **beyond the arc** again. He hit four more 3-pointers, including three in less than two minutes. Each time the ball ripped through the basket, Shaw's teammates cheered him on. With his tenth 3-point shot of the night, Shaw set a new NBA *mark*.

The Heat beat the Bucks 117–92. To a team player like Shaw, the win was far more important than his amazing record.

Legend Has It

Who has the East Coast's most glamorous basketball fans?

LEGEND HAS IT that the Heat do. For many years, they also had the NBA's most glamorous part-owner—singer Julio Iglesias. His son, Enrique, is one of the many celebrities who can be seen at Heat games. Others include actors Jamie Foxx, Courtney Cox, Sylvester Stallone, Jack Nicholson, and The Rock; singers Madonna, Gloria Estefan, Lenny Kravitz, and Jimmy Buffett; and athletes Anna Kournikova, and Jeff Gordon.

Actress Eva Longoria and Academy Award winner Jamie Foxx enjoy a Heat game.

Which team had the most fantastic finish in NBA history?

LEGEND HAS IT that the 2003–04 Heat did. The team started the season by losing seven games in a row. When the month of March began, they had 11 more losses than wins. Many fans gave up on the season. But the Heat did not. Led by **rookie** Dwyane Wade and veteran Eddie Jones, the Heat got red-hot and won 17 of their last 21 games. They ended up with 42 wins and 40 losses. No team had ever come so far—so fast—to finish with a winning record.

Eddie Jones and Dwyane Wade.

Were the Heat almost called the Miami Beaches?

LEGEND HAS IT that they were. The team's owners wanted a name that would make everyone think of Miami. The Beaches, Sharks, and Tornadoes were all names that were suggested. In the end, the team let the fans decide. They sent in more than 20,000 votes, and the winner was "Heat."

It Really Happened

Professional basketball players are trained to overcome any obstacle they face on the court. But what happens when they must fight against a life-threatening illness? In the fall of 2000, Alonzo Mourning found himself in a struggle with kidney disease. The kidneys clean the blood and help the body to work properly. Mourning's kidneys were not working correctly.

No one could believe Mourning was ill. He looked great, and seemed as strong as ever. He had just been named NBA Defensive Player of the Year, and also helped America win a gold medal in the 2000 **Summer Olympics**. Still, he was a very sick man.

Mourning's doctors tried to treat his disease with medicine. He sat out most of the 2000–01 season, then tried to play the following year. Mourning's kidneys continued to get worse. He sat out the 2002–03 season, but the rest did not help. He was told that he would die if he did not receive a kidney *transplant*.

Mourning's teammates were sad for their friend, but they knew he was a fighter. They believed that he would win this life-and-death battle. None of them, however, thought he would ever play

Alonzo Mourning's return to basketball is one of the NBA's great stories.

basketball again. Imagine their surprise when Mourning announced that he was ready to suit up in 2003–04.

Three years after he was *diagnosed* with kidney disease, Mourning was back on the court as a member of the New Jersey Nets. The following season, when the Heat needed an experienced back-up for Shaquille O'Neal, they made a trade with the Nets. Mourning returned to Miami and helped the Heat win more games than any team in the **Eastern Conference**.

Team Spirit

Miami has some of the most loyal and *passionate* fans in the country. They fill the arena and root for their team in good times and bad times. They understand what it takes to win in the NBA, and they let the Heat players know that they appreciate a job well done.

Miami is a very *diverse* city. The crowd at a Heat game is a reflection of the people who live and work in the area. As fans take their seats, you will see people who work *nine-to-five jobs* sitting next to artists, writers, and musicians. You will see retired couples chatting with young celebrities. You will see sport-fishing captains trading stories with clothing designers. You will see millionaires talking basketball with fans who can only afford to go to one or two games a year. And when the Heat score or make a great defensive play, you will see everyone—rich and poor, old and young—rising to their feet as one.

Miami fans welcome Shaquille O'Neal to the team in 2004.

Timeline

The basketball season is played from October through June. That means each season takes place at the end of one year and the beginning of the next. In this timeline, the accomplishments of the Heat are shown by season.

1988–89
The Heat play their first year in the NBA.

1993–94
The Heat win their first playoff game, against the Atlanta Hawks.

1991–92
Kevin Loughery coaches the Heat to their first playoff appearance.

1995–96
Pat Riley becomes the team's coach.

Pat Riley

Pat Riley welcomes rookie Dwyane Wade to the Heat.

1996–97
The Heat reach the Eastern Conference finals for the first time.

2003–04
Dwyane Wade makes the NBA **All-Rookie team**.

1999–2000
Alonzo Mourning is named Defensive Player of the Year for the second time.

2004–05
Shaquille O'Neal leads the Heat back to the Eastern Conference finals.

Alonzo Mourning

Shaquille O'Neal

35

Fun Facts

LONG SHOT

The first Heat player to lead the NBA in an important *statistic* was Jon Sundvold, a **reserve guard** for the team during their first season. In 1988–89, he made 52.2 percent of his 3-point shots.

BABY TALK

In 1992, the Heat drafted college star Harold Miner. Miner tried to do everything like his idol, Michael Jordan, so fans nicknamed him

"Baby Jordan." Although he made some spectacular plays, Miner could not live up to his hero. He played only four years in the NBA.

TRIPLE TROUBLE

The first player in team history to record a **triple-double** was Steve Smith. He scored 21 points with 12 assists and 10 rebounds in a game during the 1992–93 season.

Steve Smith

Glen Rice

SHOOTING STAR

Glen Rice was one of the greatest long-distance shooters in history. In 1995, he won the NBA 3-Point Shootout during All-Star Weekend in Phoenix. Two months later, he scored 56 points in a game—the highest total by any NBA player that year.

THREE THE HARD WAY

Pat Riley was NBA Coach of the Year with the Heat, New York Knicks, and Los Angeles Lakers. No one else in history has been named the league's top coach with three different teams.

LONG ARMS OF THE LAW

In December of 2005, Shaquille O'Neal fulfilled a lifelong dream. He became a reserve officer on the Miami Beach police force. He completed a one-year training course, and agreed to work for a salary of $1 a year.

Talking Hoops

Pat Riley

"There is no such thing as could-a, should-a, would-a. If you should-a and could-a...you would-a!"

—*Pat Riley, on excuses*

"You only want to use your dunks at the right time. If you do it at the right time, you can wake up everybody and change the whole ***momentum*** of the game."

—*Dwyane Wade, on the art of the slam dunk*

"There's always pressure when you come back home to play. This is the place I wanted to play. I wouldn't be where I am today if I didn't deal with pressure."

—*Eddie Jones, on being traded to his hometown of Miami*

Shaquille O'Neal

"If I was a fan, I'd come watch me play, too!"
—*Shaquille O'Neal, on why he fills up arenas wherever he plays*

"Playing defense isn't natural at all.
It's hard work if you're doing it correctly."
—*Billy Cunningham, on why the Heat's style of play is so special*

For the Record

The great Heat teams and players have left their marks on the record books. These are the "best of the best"…

Rony Seikaly

HEAT AWARD WINNERS

WINNER	AWARD	SEASON
Rony Seikaly	Most Improved Player	1989–90
Harold Miner	Slam Dunk Champion	1992–93
Harold Miner	Slam Dunk Champion	1994–95
Glen Rice	3-Point Shootout Winner	1994–95
Isaac Austin	Most Improved Player	1996–97
Pat Riley	Coach of the Year	1996–97
Alonzo Mourning	Defensive Player of the Year	1998–99
Alonzo Mourning	Defensive Player of the Year	1999–00

Hall of Famer Bill Russell congratulates Alonzo Mourning on his Defensive Player of the Year award.

HEAT ACHIEVEMENT

ACHIEVEMENT	SEASON
Atlantic Division Champions	1996–97
Atlantic Division Champions	1997–98
Atlantic Division Champions	1998–99
Atlantic Division Champions	1999–00
Southeast Division Champions	2004–05

TOP: Coach of the Year Pat Riley.
ABOVE: All-Star Dwyane Wade.
LEFT: Dan Majerle enjoys a Miami playoff win.

Pinpoints

The history of a basketball team is made up of many smaller stories. These stories take place all over the map—not just in the city a team calls "home." Match the push-pins on these maps to the Team Facts and you will begin to see the story of the Heat unfold!

TEAM FACTS

1 Miami, Florida—*The Heat have played here since 1988–89.*

2 Chesapeake, Virginia—*Alonzo Mourning was born here.*

3 Newark, New Jersey—*Shaquille O'Neal was born here.*

4 Brooklyn, New York—*Billy Cunningham was born here.*

5 Rome, New York—*Pat Riley was born here.*

6 Columbus, Ohio—*Brian Grant was born here.*

7 Flint, Michigan—*Glen Rice was born here.*

8 Chicago, Illinois—*Dwyane Wade was born here.*

9 Los Angeles, California—*The Heat won their first game here.*

10 Phoenix, Arizona—*Glen Rice won the 1995 3-Point Shootout here.*

11 Tel Aviv, Israel—*Mickey Arison was born here.*

12 Beirut, Lebanon—*Rony Seikaly was born here.*

Brian Grant, the team's top rebounder in 2002–03.

Play Ball

Basketball is a sport played by two teams of five players. NBA games have four 12-minute quarters—48 minutes in all—and the team that scores the most points when time has run out is the winner. Most baskets count for two points. Players who make shots from beyond the three-point line receive an extra point. Baskets made from the free-throw line count for one point. Free throws are penalty shots awarded to a team, usually after an opponent has committed a foul. A foul is called when one player makes hard contact with another.

Players can move around all they want, but the player with the ball cannot. He must bounce the ball with one hand or the other (but never both) in order to go from one part of the court to another. As long as he keeps "dribbling," he can keep moving.

In the NBA, teams must attempt a shot every 24 seconds, so there is little time to waste. The job of the defense is to make it as difficult as possible to take a good shot—and to grab the ball if the other team shoots and misses.

This may sound simple, but anyone who has played the game knows that basketball can be very complicated. Every player on the court has a job to do. Different players have different strengths and weaknesses. The coach must mix these players in just the right way, and teach them to work together as one.

The more you play and watch basketball, the more "little things" you are likely to notice. The next time you are at a game, look for these plays:

PLAY LIST

ALLEY-OOP—A play where the passer throws the ball just to the side of the rim—so a teammate can catch it and dunk in one motion.

BACK-DOOR PLAY—A play where the passer waits for his teammate to fake the defender away from the basket—then throws him the ball when he cuts back toward the basket.

KICK-OUT—A play where the ball-handler waits for the defense to surround him—then quickly passes to a teammate who is open for an outside shot. The ball is not really kicked in this play; the term comes from the action of pinball machines.

NO-LOOK PASS—A play where the passer fools a defender (with his eyes) into covering one teammate—then suddenly passes to another without looking.

PICK-AND-ROLL—A play where one teammate blocks or "picks off" another's defender with his body—then cuts to the basket for a pass in the confusion.

Glossary

BASKETBALL WORDS TO KNOW

3-POINT LINE—The boundary that separates a 2-point shot from a 3-point shot.

ALL-NBA—An honor given to the NBA's best players at the end of the season.

ALL-ROOKIE TEAM—A group of the best first-year players honored at the end of the season.

ALL-STAR GAME—A game played each year between two teams made up of the league's best players.

AMERICAN BASKETBALL ASSOCIATION (ABA)—A basketball league that played for nine seasons, beginning in 1967. Prior to the 1976–77 season, four ABA teams joined the NBA, and the rest went out of business.

ASSISTS—Passes that lead to successful shots.

AVERAGED—Made an average of.

BEYOND THE ARC—Outside the 3-point line.

DECIDING GAME—The last game of a series that is tied.

DIVISION—A group of teams that play in the same part of the country.

DRAFTED—Picked from a group of the best college players.

DRIVE—Move strongly towards the basket.

EASTERN CONFERENCE—One of two conferences that make up the NBA; the champions of the Eastern and Western Conferences play in the NBA Finals.

HALL OF FAME—The place where the game's greatest players are honored; these players are often called "Hall of Famers."

NATIONAL BASKETBALL ASSOCIATION (NBA)—The professional league that has been operating since the 1946–47 season.

NBA FINALS—The playoff series which decides the championship of the league.

PLAYMAKER—A player who helps teammates score with good passes.

POINT GUARD—The player who runs the offense for a basketball team.

RESERVE GUARD—A guard who begins the game on the bench.

ROLE PLAYER—Someone who is asked to do specific things when he is in a game.

ROOKIE—A player in his first season.

SHOOTING PERCENTAGE—The percentage of shots that go in the basket.

SUPPORTING ROLES—Jobs that enable a team's stars to perform at their best.

SUMMER OLYMPICS—The international sports competition held every four years.

TIP-OFF—The jump ball that starts a game.

TRIPLE-DOUBLE—Ten or more points, rebounds, and assists (or blocks or steals) in the same game.

OTHER WORDS TO KNOW

ACQUIRE—To buy or trade for.

AT STAKE—At risk.

DIAGNOSED—Told by a doctor about an illness or injury.

CAMPAIGN—A series of actions meant to achieve a goal.

DIVERSE—All kinds of people.

INVESTED—Risked money hoping to make a profit.

LAID-BACK—Casual and easygoing.

MARK—Record.

MOMENTUM—Strength of movement.

NINE-TO-FIVE JOBS—Jobs where people report to work at 9:00 A.M. and leave at 5:00 P.M.

PASSIONATE—Having strong emotions.

REAL ESTATE—Land with a building on it.

SATIN—A smooth, shiny fabric.

STATISTIC—A number measuring an action or accomplishment.

SYNTHETIC—Made in a laboratory, not in nature.

TRADITION—A belief or custom that is handed down from generation to generation.

TRANSPLANT—An operation in which an organ is moved from one body to another.

Places to Go

ON THE ROAD

AMERICAN AIRLINES ARENA
601 Biscayne Boulevard
Miami, Florida 33132
(786) 777-HEAT

NAISMITH MEMORIAL BASKETBALL HALL OF FAME
1000 West Columbus Avenue
Springfield, MA 01105
(877) 4HOOPLA

ON THE WEB

THE NATIONAL BASKETBALL ASSOCIATION   www.nba.com
  • *to learn more about the league's teams, players, and history*

THE MIAMI HEAT   www.Heat.com
  • *to learn more about the Miami Heat*

THE BASKETBALL HALL OF FAME   www.hoophall.com
  • *to learn more about history's greatest players*

ON THE BOOKSHELF

To learn more about the sport of basketball, look for these books at your library or bookstore:
  • Burgan, Michael. *Great Moments in Basketball.* New York, NY.: World Almanac, 2002.
  • Ingram, Scott. *A Basketball All-Star.* Chicago, IL.: Heinemann Library, 2005.
  • Suen, Anastasia. *The Story of Basketball.* New York, NY.: PowerKids Press, 2002.

Index

The Team

MARK STEWART has written more than 20 books on basketball, and over 100 sports books for kids. He grew up in New York City during the 1960s rooting for the Knicks and Nets, and now takes his two daughters, Mariah and Rachel, to watch them play. Mark comes from a family of writers. His grandfather was Sunday Editor of *The New York Times* and his mother was Articles Editor of *The Ladies Home Journal* and *McCall's*. Mark has profiled hundreds of athletes over the last 20 years. He has also written several books about his native New York, and New Jersey, his home today. Mark is a graduate of Duke University, with a degree in history. He lives with his daughters and wife, Sarah, overlooking Sandy Hook, NJ.

MATT ZEYSING is the resident historian at the Basketball Hall of Fame in Springfield, Massachusetts. His research interests include the origins of the game of basketball, the development of professional basketball in the first half of the twentieth century, and the culture and meaning of basketball in American society.

HEROES OF AMERICAN HISTORY

Clara Barton

Brave Nurse

Carin T. Ford

Enslow Elementary

an imprint of

Enslow Publishers, Inc.
40 Industrial Road
Box 398
Berkeley Heights, NJ 07922
USA

http://www.enslow.com

Enslow Elementary, an imprint of Enslow Publishers, Inc.

Enslow Elementary® is a registered trademark of Enslow Publishers, Inc.

Library of Congress Cataloging-in-Publication Data

Ford, Carin T.
    Clara Barton : brave nurse / Carin T. Ford.
       p. cm. — (Heroes of American history)
    Includes index.
    ISBN 0-7660-2602-7 (hardcover)
    1. Barton, Clara, 1821–1912—Juvenile literature. 2. American Red Cross—Biography—Juvenile literature. 3. Nurses—United States—Biography—Juvenile literature. I. Title. II. Series.
    HV569.B3F67 2006
    361.7'634'092—dc22
                                                   2005009503

Printed in the United States of America

10 9 8 7 6 5 4 3 2 1

To Our Readers: We have done our best to make sure all Internet Addresses in this book were active and appropriate when we went to press. However, the author and the publisher have no control over and assume no liability for the material available on those Internet sites or on other Web sites they may link to. Any comments or suggestions can be sent by e-mail to comments@enslow.com or to the address on the back cover.

Every effort has been made to locate all copyright holders of material used in this book. If any errors or omissions have occurred, corrections will be made in future editions of this book.

Illustration Credits: © 2004 Hemera Technologies, Inc., p. 9; American Red Cross, pp. 3, 4, 13, 15; AP/Wide World, pp. 7, 8, 23 (T), 29 (L); The Architect of the Capitol, p. 22; Clara Barton Birthplace Museum, pp. 6, 21; Courtesy of the Clara Barton National Historic Site, National Park Service, p. 29; Enslow Publishers, pp. 2, 17 (L), 23 (B), 25; Library of Congress, pp. 11, 12, 16, 17 (R), 20, 26, 27, 29 (T); Northwind Picture Archives, pp. 18, 28; Portrait Artist: Daniel E. Greene. Portrait photo courtesy Mechanics Hall, Worcester, MA., p. 1.

Cover Illustrations: Portrait Artist: Daniel E. Greene. Portrait photo courtesy Mechanics Hall, Worcester, MA. (detail). Background: The Architect of the Capitol.

Table of Contents

Clara Barton

Chapter 1

Shy Child

Clarissa Harlowe Barton was born on Christmas Day, 1821, in North Oxford, Massachusetts. Her parents, Stephen and Sarah, already had four children: Dorothy, age seventeen; Stephen, fifteen; David, thirteen; and Sally, ten. The Bartons had many nicknames for baby Clarissa. They called her Tot, Tabitha, Baby, Clary, and Clara.

Clara's mother worked hard caring for her family.

Stephen and Sarah Barton, Clara's parents.

She had a bad temper and screamed a lot. Clara was a shy little girl, scared of everything from thunderstorms to snakes. "I remember nothing but fear," she once said about her childhood.

Clara's father had been a soldier, and he told stories about fighting against American Indians in the West. When no river was nearby, he had to drink muddy water from a horse's hoofprint so he would not die of thirst. Clara liked to sit on his knee as he talked about American Indians and their tomahawks and arrows. She called him her "soldier father."

To Clara, it seemed as if she had six parents, because her brothers and sisters were so much older. They helped take care of her and taught her many things. Clara learned how to ride horses, throw a ball, and skip stones across a creek. Before long, she was reading, spelling, and doing math problems.

Clara started school when she was three. She rode there on her older brother's shoulders. On the first day, Clara's teacher was

Clara was born in this house. Today, it is a museum.

BIRTHPLACE OF
CLARA BARTON
FOUNDER OF THE
AMERICAN RED CROSS

A peek inside the Barton house shows her mother's spinning wheel.

surprised that such a little girl could already read and spell long words like "artichoke."

Clara was a good student. Most families at that time did not think it was important for girls to get much schooling. But Clara's family was very proud of her. When Clara was eight, they sent her to a boarding school, hoping it would cure her shyness. But the plan did not work. Clara said she worried all the time about "doing something wrong." She was so homesick that she would not talk or eat. After a few weeks, she was sent home.

About that time, Clara's family moved to a farm. Clara's cousins also lived there, and she liked playing with two of the younger boys. The children jumped off high wooden boards in the barn, landing on piles of hay. They hiked through fields and hills, explored caves, and played hide-and-seek. Clara helped with the farm chores. She learned how to milk cows, fix broken fences, and paint walls. She fed the ducks, chickens, and cats. One of the dogs, named Button, was her own special pet.

Chapter 2

Young Nurse

One day in 1832, Clara's brother David was helping to build a new roof for the barn. Crash! David fell off the roof. He got a bad headache and came down with a fever. In those days, doctors did not have the medicines we have today. The doctor told the family to put leeches on David's skin. A leech is a kind of worm that sucks blood.

Clara, age eleven, became David's nurse. At first,

she said, the leeches seemed like "so many snakes."
But soon she lost her fear. Clara liked being David's
nurse, and she stayed at his bedside to
take care of him. "I almost forgot that
there was an outside to the house,"
she said. Finally, after almost two
years, the doctors said the leeches
were not helping. Without them,
David got better at last.

For a short time, Clara went
back to school. She was a top
student in chemistry, Latin, and
other subjects. But most of all, Clara
liked doing things for other people.

David was Clara's
favorite brother.

She looked after her sister Sally's children, helped
poor children with their schoolwork, and nursed sick
people in town.

Yet Clara was still very shy, and she cried a lot.

Her parents did not know what to do. A visitor to the Barton house said that Clara might make a good teacher. The family agreed that she should try.

Clara was seventeen when she got her first job as a teacher. She felt scared at the idea of standing in front of a classroom. She was very small and wanted

All of Clara's students sat in the same room, as in this one-room schoolhouse.

to look taller and older. So she wore long skirts and piled her hair high on her head.

Clara as a young schoolteacher.

The school had forty students of all ages, from toddlers to teens. On the first day, Clara was too shy to talk to the class. Instead, she read from the Bible. Before long, Clara had become a wonderful teacher. She made learning fun for the children. Even the older boys admired Clara because she could throw a ball better than they could.

Clara taught at different schools for ten years. She was not shy anymore. In fact, Clara was learning how to stand up for what she wanted. One school did not want to pay her as much as they paid men. "I shall never do a man's work for less than a man's pay," she told them. After that, they paid her more money.

Chapter 3

Finding Ways to Help

C lara went back to school in 1851 to learn more. That same year, she got the sad news that her mother had died.

When Clara was done with her schooling, she did not know what to do next. She went to New Jersey to visit some friends. In Bordentown, she saw many children out in the streets. Why were they not in school? "There is no school for us," they said. The local schools cost money, and their families were too poor to pay.

Clara opened a free school in 1852. It was such a success that the next year, the town built a brand-new school. It was big enough for six hundred students. Then they hired a man to be the principal. A woman could not be in charge, they said. Clara knew that was not right. She was angry and upset.

Clara, age twenty-nine.

In 1854 Clara moved to Washington, D.C. She took a job in a government office and worked there off and on for the next few years. In those days, most office jobs were held by men. It was rare for women to go out to work. Their job was to take care of their homes and children. Once again, Clara boldly spoke out for the rights of women to be equal to men.

By 1860, the United States was on the brink of war. Trouble was brewing between states in the North and states in the South. Many people, mostly in the South, owned slaves. Slaves were not treated like people. Instead, they were bought and sold like property. They were forced to work for no pay. The huge farms in the South needed many slaves to grow cotton. People in the South were worried: What if the new president, Abraham Lincoln, put an end to slavery?

Some states in the South took action: They said they were starting their own country called the Confederate States of America. But President Lincoln did not want the United States to split in two—and he was ready to fight to keep the country

President Lincoln

Union states and territories

Confederate states and territories

Border states (slave states that sided with the Union)

West Virginia*
*Separated from Virginia in 1861 and joined the Union in 1863

In the Civil War, soldiers from the North (the Union) fought against soldiers from the South (the Confederacy).

together. War broke out between the North and the South in 1861.

Men from the North came to Washington, D.C., to join Lincoln's army. The southerners were angry. They yelled and threw bricks at the new soldiers. When Clara saw men who were hurt, she hurried to help. She filled baskets with needles, thread, scissors, pens,

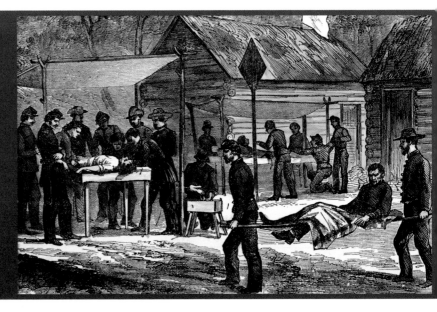

Often, wounded men were treated on tables set up near the battlefields.

soap, and buttons. She tore up old sheets for towels. Clara took jellies, pies, and cakes to the soldiers.

Two weeks later, fighting broke out nearby in Virginia. Clara handed out food and clothing to the Union soldiers. She stroked the heads of wounded men and wrote letters for them. She called them her "boys."

Clara was not afraid of war. She said she felt ready "to face danger, but never *fear* it." Clara was glad to help. It made her feel good: "While our soldiers can stand and *fight*, I can stand and feed and nurse them."

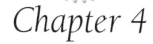

Chapter 4

"Angel of the Battlefield"

Clara put ads in newspapers asking people to give money and supplies to the Union soldiers. She spent plenty of her own money, too. Soon, Clara had lots of supplies. She filled a horse-drawn wagon and drove it to the battlefront. "That's no place for a lady," an officer told her. "There's going to be a battle."

"But that is why I want to be there," said Clara. When the officer found out that Clara had food and medicine, he let her go. After that, she was often on the battlefield during the Civil War. Bullets whizzed by and even tore her clothing. But Clara sang cheerfully as she cooked food, brought water to Union soldiers, and held the heads of suffering men. The soldiers called her the "Angel of the Battlefield."

Clara gave this soldier a drink of water on the battlefield.

At a battle in Fredericksburg, Virginia, in 1862, Clara cared for some enemy prisoners. It was so cold that their bloody clothing had frozen to the ground and had to be chopped away with an ax. She wrapped the soldiers in blankets and gave them warm drinks.

Two years later, Clara was working in hospital tents in Virginia. She slept on a straw bed on a dirt floor. One night, she came upon a boy whose shoulder was badly hurt. He was scared that he would die. Clara sat with him through the night. She talked gently and gave him medicine. As the soldier got better, he told her, "I would have died had it not been for you."

Clara nursed men in tents, churches, hotels, and houses. She went wherever the army put its wounded soldiers.

When the war ended in 1865,

there too weak to eat, — a boiled egg for there who could — but most of all the bread and butter. Men with shattered limbs, shot through and through, — think of them — men raised among all the comforts of a Northern home — with the tears of gratitude rolling over their faces at the mere fact of a piece of soft bread with butter on it: — "Butter! Madam. I has n't tasted butter in eight months." And to see strong men, manly — educated men, gnawing off the butter side like little children and holding out the ragged slice with poor cold bloody fingers for a "little" more butter, please," Oh how the gloom of the night wore away, and their poor hearts lightened with only there little helps, and finally as it came day light, and they had slept and

21

So many men were hurt during the Civil War
that rooms in the Capitol in Washington, D.C.,
had to be used as a hospital.

Clara found another way to help. Many soldiers were missing. Families did not know if their loved ones were alive or dead.

Clara set up an office to find these missing men. She wrote down the soldiers' names and sent the lists to newspapers. She also put up lists in post offices. If people knew about someone on the list, they would tell Clara. By 1869, she had found out what happened to 22,000 of the missing men.

Clara gave speeches to raise money for the work she was doing. But she was always very nervous in front of groups of people. "All speech-making terrifies me," she said. ". . . I hate it."

Chapter 5

The American Red Cross

Clara was very tired from all her work. Her doctor said she needed to rest. So Clara went to Europe with her sister. When they visited Switzerland, Clara learned about the International Red Cross. Workers for this group helped take care of soldiers during war times.

France went to war against Germany in 1870—and once again, Clara went to work. She joined the Red Cross and helped people who had lost their homes because of the war. Both France and Germany honored her when the war ended three years later.

Clara returned to the United States in 1873. She wanted to start a Red Cross in America. Clara met with lawmakers in Washington, D.C., about setting up the Red Cross. She wanted the American Red Cross to help not only during wars, but also during disasters such as floods, fires, and terrible storms.

Finally, on May 21, 1881, the American Red Cross was founded. A few weeks later, Clara was voted in as president of the group.

For the next twenty years, Clara set up Red Cross projects around the country. The Red Cross rebuilt homes that were burned in a Michigan forest fire. Workers took medical supplies to a New York town

The American Red Cross helps people in need.

1. Carts of food in the 1880s saved hungry people in South Carolina.
2. Potatoes for planting helped Georgia farmers in 1893.
3. & 4. A hurricane in 1900 caused damage in Galveston, Texas.

where people suffered from a deadly disease. When a tornado destroyed homes in Illinois, the Red Cross gave food and clothing to three thousand homeless people.

When Clara was in her eighties, she wrote two books, *A Story of the Red Cross* and *The Story of My Childhood*. She also went to meetings of old Civil War soldiers and women's rights groups. At that time, only men were allowed to vote. Clara was a strong believer in giving women the right to vote. When a friend urged Clara to rest, she said, "Are you in your right mind to ask *me* to rest?"

Clara died on April 12, 1912. She was ninety years old. Clara devoted her life to helping others. Today, the American Red Cross carries on her work. More than one million Americans volunteer their time to help the Red Cross every year.

All her life,
Clara worked
hard to help
other people.

Timeline

1821~Clara is born in North Oxford, Massachusetts on December 25.

1839~Begins teaching.

1854~Moves to Washington, D.C., and works in a government office.

1861~Helps first wounded soldiers in Civil War.

1865~Identifies soldiers missing in Civil War.

1869~In Europe, learns of the International Red Cross.

1881~Starts the American Red Cross and becomes its president.

1904~Publishes *A Story of the Red Cross*.

1912~Dies in Glen Echo, Maryland, on April 12.

Words to Know

American Civil War—A four-year war (1861–1865) between the southern and northern states of the United States of America.

boarding school—A school where students live while they attend classes.

international—For two or more nations, or countries.

Latin—The language used by Romans a long time ago.

leech—A kind of blood-sucking worm that doctors used to believe could cure patients by removing "bad" blood. But the leeches made patients weaker because of the blood loss.

tomahawk—A small ax that Native Americans used as tools or weapons.

volunteer—To do work for free, often to help others.

Learn More

Books

Collier, James Lincoln. *The Clara Barton You Never Knew*. New York: Children's Press, 2003.

Deady, Kathleen W. *Clara Barton, a Photo-Illustrated Biography*. Mankato, Minn.: Capstone Press, 2003.

Ransom, Candace. *Clara Barton*. Minneapolis, Minn.: Lerner Publications, 2003.

Internet Addresses

American Red Cross—a timeline.
   <http://www.redcross.org/museum/timemach.html>

Clara Barton—Angel of the Battlefield.
   <http://www.nps.government/anti/clara.htm>

Clara Barton biography.
   <http://www.civilwarhome.com/bartonbio.htm>

Index